Time - An Enigma

Louise Altman

BookLeaf Publishing

India | USA | UK

Presentation by *BookLeaf Publishing*

Web: www.bookleafpub.com

E-mail: info@bookleafpub.com

ISBN : 9789357447911

First edition 2021

DEDICATION

These poems are dedicated to all the
Australians locked out of their country during
the hardest times of our lives. We are strong.
We will persevere.

The Theory of Nothing

Time
An incomprehensible enigma.
I'm sure if Stephen Hawking were here, he'd be
able to explain it to me,
However-
Please excuse the overly cliché idiom here,
His time is up in this earthly, existential crisis
inducing coil.
So
I guess I'll have to figure it out by myself.

Do You?

Do you remember as a child, summer would last forever?
Do you remember days out in the sun riding bikes and skateboards?
Do you remember making tree houses?
Do you remember playing in water parks where we washed all the sunscreen off going down the water slides and then leaving at the end of the day with t-shirts sticking to our tender pink skin?
Do you?

Calendar Motions

Have you ever noticed that as an adult, life
seems to speed up?
We count down for the beginning of a new year
Suddenly it's July
We fly through to August
Question how we made it to November
and then
Suddenly we're counting down to the next New
Year.
All to do it over again.

I don't want you

I didn't notice how quickly Time consumed
everything in my life, until I had too much of it.
Until it became this
Overwhelming
Unwanted
Presence that overshadowed every moment -
waking and sleeping - in my existence.

Zest

The friendship between humans and Time is
already quite testy.
We love it as a child,
We crave it as a young adult,
We question its motives as we move into the
years of our mid-life crises,
We loathe it when we enter the final stages.

It takes everything from us; our mental facilities,
our physical capabilities – we become
incapacitated by an abundance of nothing that
suspends us in a state of putrefaction.
And then it's over.
If you're lucky you'll get a good eighty years of
functionality.
If you're not, you'll either get much less, or
much more.
The latter doesn't sound so ominous, that is until
you become plagued with dementia,
Alzheimer's, or a general lack of zest for the
living…

Sweet, Sweet Irony

The irony is thus: we demand that Time makes
all the rules,
And then we don't want to follow them.
We set alarms to wake us up at a particular time.
We spend time traveling to work.
We spend a mandated period of time at said
work,
Then our leisure activities are dictated by the
amount of time we can either spend doing them,
Or not.
We even count the hours of sleep we get, in
order to achieve the perfect amount of time in a
semi-conscious state.

Stagnating

Much of my 2020 was spent locked inside a flat,
unable to go out, with the only activities to fill
the time, being:
Work,
Cooking,
Eating,
Watching obscene amounts of Netflix,
The entire Simpsons catalogue,
And waiting for someone in another time-zone
to wake up and entertain the mundane that had
become my life.

One minute felt like ten, twenty minutes felt like
hours.
I don't think there has been a time where I have
been so ashamed of the person I became while
waiting – stagnating – for someone else to
entertain me, to talk to me, to give me mental
stimulation.

Mutual Decomposition

In a sense I used them.
They were the product of a conversation, that
materialized into a continuing of life as we knew
it before the world changed,
And plenty of unrealistic hopes for the future.
Only,
Time became a reaper of that relationship with
that person.
They didn't have enough time to grieve,
And I became the victim that they fixated on,
And then the festering limb they needed to cut
off in order to heal and grow.

Broken Hearts

I don't blame them.
I don't blame them for doing that.
The removal was the natural course that
probably needed to happen for them.
I do however blame myself for becoming
attached to an idea,
A dream,
A promise – one which was only given under
false pretenses.
I don't blame them.

Goodbye

The cessation of conversation
Felt like the moment you feel pin pricks
stabbing into your face as someone throws a
bucket of ice-cold water over you.
Either in jest or malice,
The result is the same.
You end up mildly damp, your hair gets ruined,
if you're lucky your makeup stays on your face,
and you get goosebumps from the frozen fingers
of the breeze that tangles itself around your
neck.

Weary

The numbness sets in and takes hold like a
weary traveler settling into shelter during a
storm.
You struggle to remain a functioning member of
society as you slowly but surely feel yourself
becoming paralyzed by the lack of movement
– the toing and froing of conversation,
The challenge of deciding whether or not that
person is a good fit for you as you learn and
discover more about them.
Time, the inglorious bastard that it is, decided to
freeze in that moment.
To take a pause and watch the damage that it had
wreaked over my life.
The stillness, the silence, it was devastatingly
loud.

Despite

Then I met you.
When we grow up and get married,
Can we please have babies and puppies, and
chickens and duckies?
Our lives are already chaotic and messy but let's
just make do with the time we've got together.
Time is fleeting and the clock is counting down,
but all I know is that despite the chaos, despite
the stagnation, despite the hell we've already
gone through,
You are a breath of fresh air that is finally
helping me to breathe.
I may have lost myself somewhere in the middle
of all this, but I'm slowly coming back.
You're helping me to come back.

Who am I?

What is one thing that I want to be?
I want to always be unashamedly myself.
There is no other person in the world I would
rather be.
That is not to say that some days I abhor the way
I look or feel about certain people or things
including myself, because there are also days
where I adore myself too, and wouldn't change a
thing.
What I mean is that if I lived a life that was so
drastically different from the life that I have- that
I have crafted for myself using the Time that I
was allotted,
I wouldn't be me.
I don't know who I would be, but it's certainly
not the woman who is sat at her little hotel desk,
alone in her quarantine room for 14 days, hair
freshly washed at 1am, and drank peppermint
tea at 4am because of jetlag.

Decisions

I laugh a little too loudly.
I can be seen as a very obnoxious and spiteful
person;
I crave alone time and hate conversation in the
morning without a hot cup of coffee at hand.
I take photos and ask to have photos taken of me
– I never used to do that.
I listen to music that people have suggested,
even if I don't like the genre because it shows
me a little more of what that person likes.
I eat an unhealthy amount of chocolate and don't
brush my teeth enough to justify it.
I stress bite my nails unconsciously, but don't
want to inconvenience any one because of
something I have done.
I hate asking for help because it means that a
part of me has to be vulnerable.

But I like being vulnerable with the right people.
I give love recklessly and bravely, and wear
sunflower earrings just because they brighten up
the room.
I am in no way a one hundred percent loveable
person, but I am a person who loves; and that's
fine with me.

I've used my allotted amount of Time to decide
on that.

15

Nothing

Nothing.
Nothing prepares you for the emptiness that washes over you when you have something life altering taken away.
Nothing prepares you for the build up, the anticipation.
There are the nervous, sleepless nights where you lie either by yourself in a pool of anxiety sweats,
Or next to someone you love, trying not to move around too much to wake them up.
There's the unhealthy coffee and tea drinking habits,
The lack of eating food that is enough to be considered a healthy and sustainable diet.
There's the random panics thinking that something is going to go wrong, but then you have to reassure yourself that everything is going to be ok, and whatever happens is going to happen whether you like it or not.
However you look at it, next week will arrive at exactly the same time irrespective of how you occupy your time, no matter how good or bad that week was.
Nothing prepares you.

Nothing.

The Moment

The moment that Time stops,
The moment where he becomes the vengeful
god that decides how long you live in the
suspension of nothing,
That is the moment
When everything
Goes
To hell.

My Void

He made me live in my void for a solid minute
before the Earth started turning again.
That minute was the longest minute of my life;
Before my lungs constricted and forcibly sucked
air into my body and made me realise that tears
had cascaded down my cheeks,
And someone was calling my name to ask if I
was ok.

Scars

My moment is scarred with the scent of sheep in
a paddock,
The lingering, semi-stale smell of a shirt that is
one too many days past it's to be washed use-by
date,
And bacon frying in a pan over a camping stove.
This is the moment that will be triggered by
PTSD flashbacks.
One day when I smell bacon cooking,
Or walk out into a paddock,
Or even do my washing,
I will be transported back to the time where
Time made me live in an overabundance of
nothing.

It's All Up For Interpretation

Hope is reassuring and beautiful and all things good,
Blah,
Blah,
Blah.

It's also the most debilitating force in the existence of the universe.
Take someone's hope away and they become an empty shell of the person they once used to be. Almost a festering carcass that on the outside still looks ok, but on the inside is full of decomposition and decay that is too far gone to be saved.
That's my interpretation of being hopeless.
After my hope was dismantled in the eternal minute that will live in my mind for the rest of my days, the next emotion to plague me was fear.

I Was

I was afraid to be by myself; to be left with the cacophony that was constantly creating chaos in my mind.
It was a messy place to be,
My thoughts,
And he helped me keep the hoarded boxes of anxieties and fears from falling down on me.

"When are you going to pick me up from this existential hell?"
"I'll be there at five thirty. Go enjoy a drink with your friend. Get out of the flat, get some fresh air. Remember, I love you."

The kindness that this man showed me when I was a mess still fills me with warmth.
I was afraid to be by myself because I couldn't think of what to do next without someone else validating my choice, just in case it was the wrong one.
I was frozen with fear of not being able to be good enough to make the right choices at the right time.

I was scared of being alone in a country that was
not my own, but one I had simply borrowed for
two years.
I was scared because my own country didn't
want me back.
Now what would happen?

Lucky?

Not knowing when or how I was going to come
home was a petrifying ordeal. The sad thing is
that I wasn't the only person feeling that.
There were, and still are, tens of thousands of
Australians who had been let down by their
country.
We'd been stranded.
I was one of the lucky ones.
With that knowledge comes a certain amount of
guilt that I haven't properly had the time to
process, despite being inundated by an
abundance of it.
Lucky doesn't feel so lucky
With all this time to think about it.